THE ART OF THE OCEAN

2025 CALENDAR

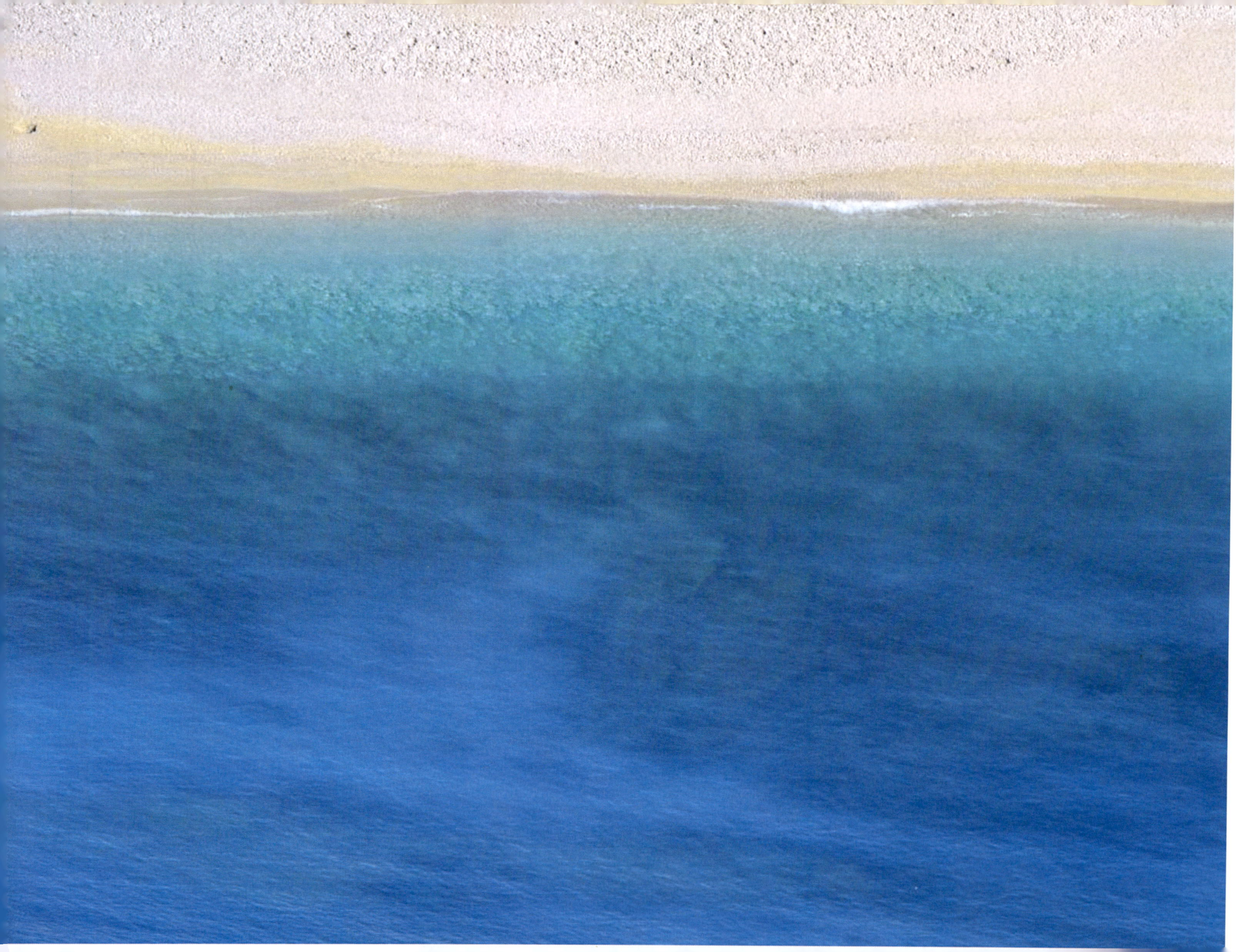

JANUARY 2025

SUNDAY	MONDAY	TUESDAY	WEDNESDAY	THURSDAY	FRIDAY	SATURDAY
29	30	31	1	2	3	4
5	6	7	8	9	10	11
12	13	14	15	16	17	18
19	20	21	22	23	24	25
26	27	28	29	30	31	1

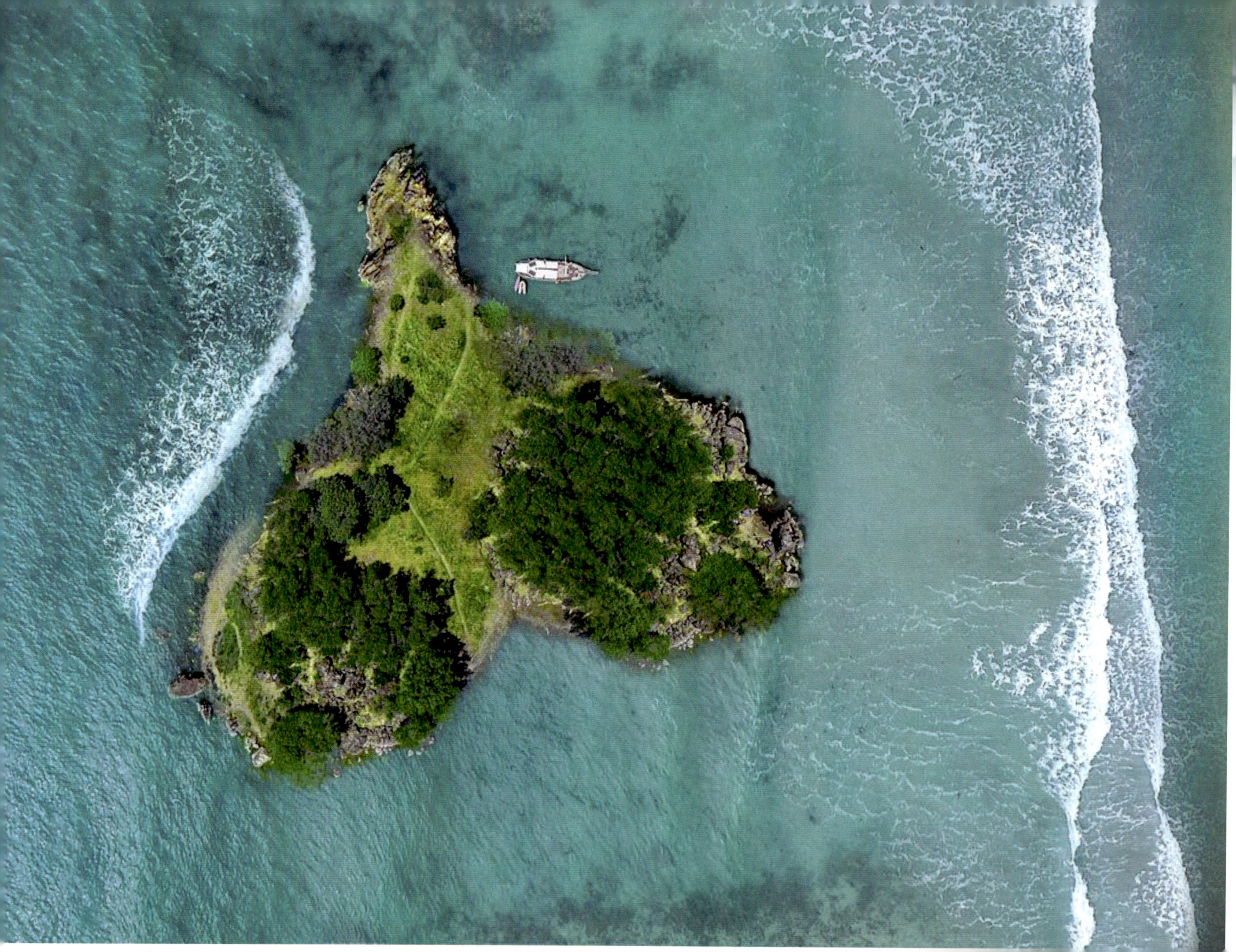

FEBRUARY 2025

SUNDAY	MONDAY	TUESDAY	WEDNESDAY	THURSDAY	FRIDAY	SATURDAY
26	27	28	29	30	31	1
2	3	4	5	6	7	8
9	10	11	12	13	14	15
16	17	18	19	20	21	22
23	24	25	26	27	28	1

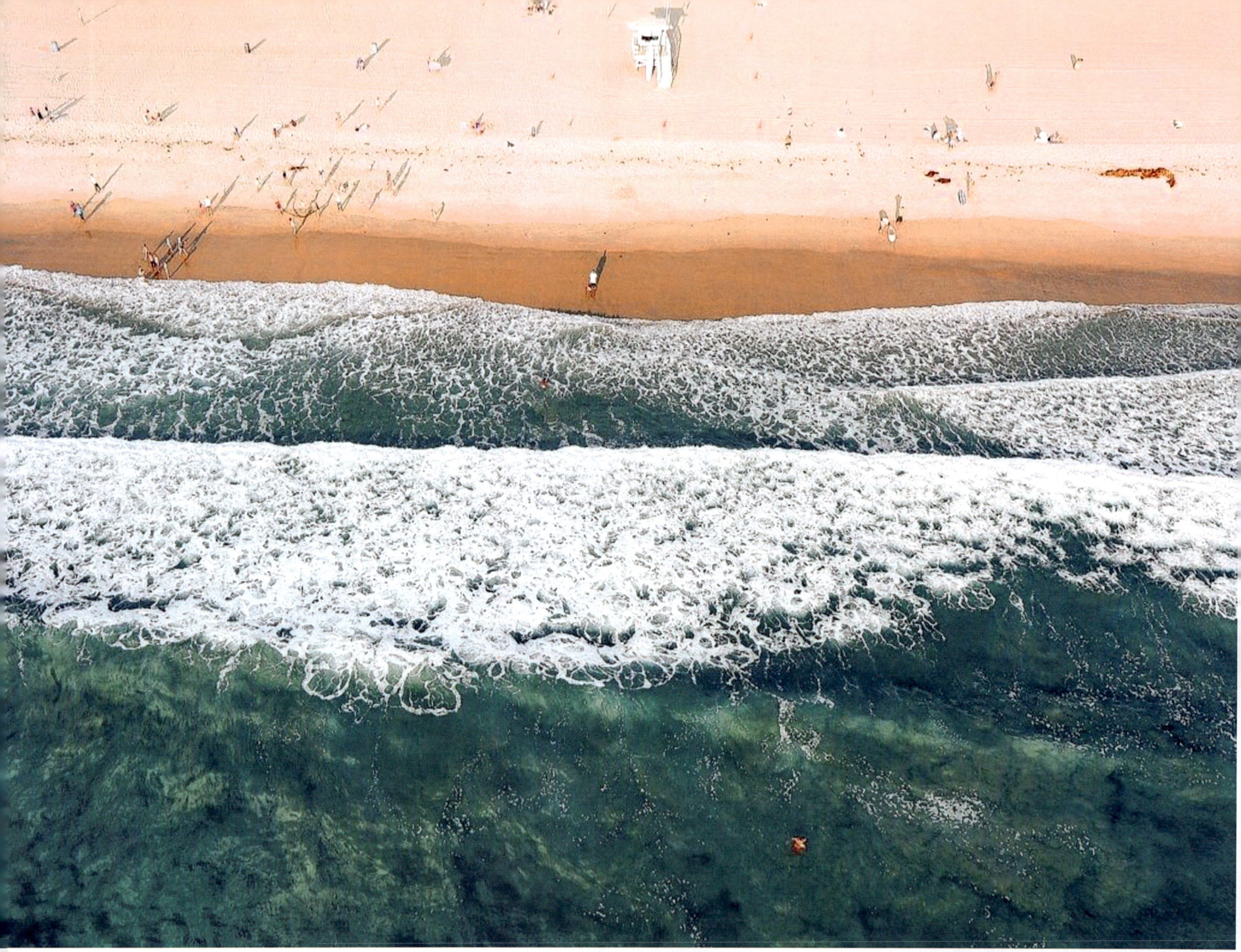

MARCH 2025

SUNDAY	MONDAY	TUESDAY	WEDNESDAY	THURSDAY	FRIDAY	SATURDAY
23	24	25	26	27	28	1
2	3	4	5	6	7	8
9	10	11	12	13	14	15
16	17	18	19	20	21	22
23 / 30	24 / 31	25	26	27	28	29

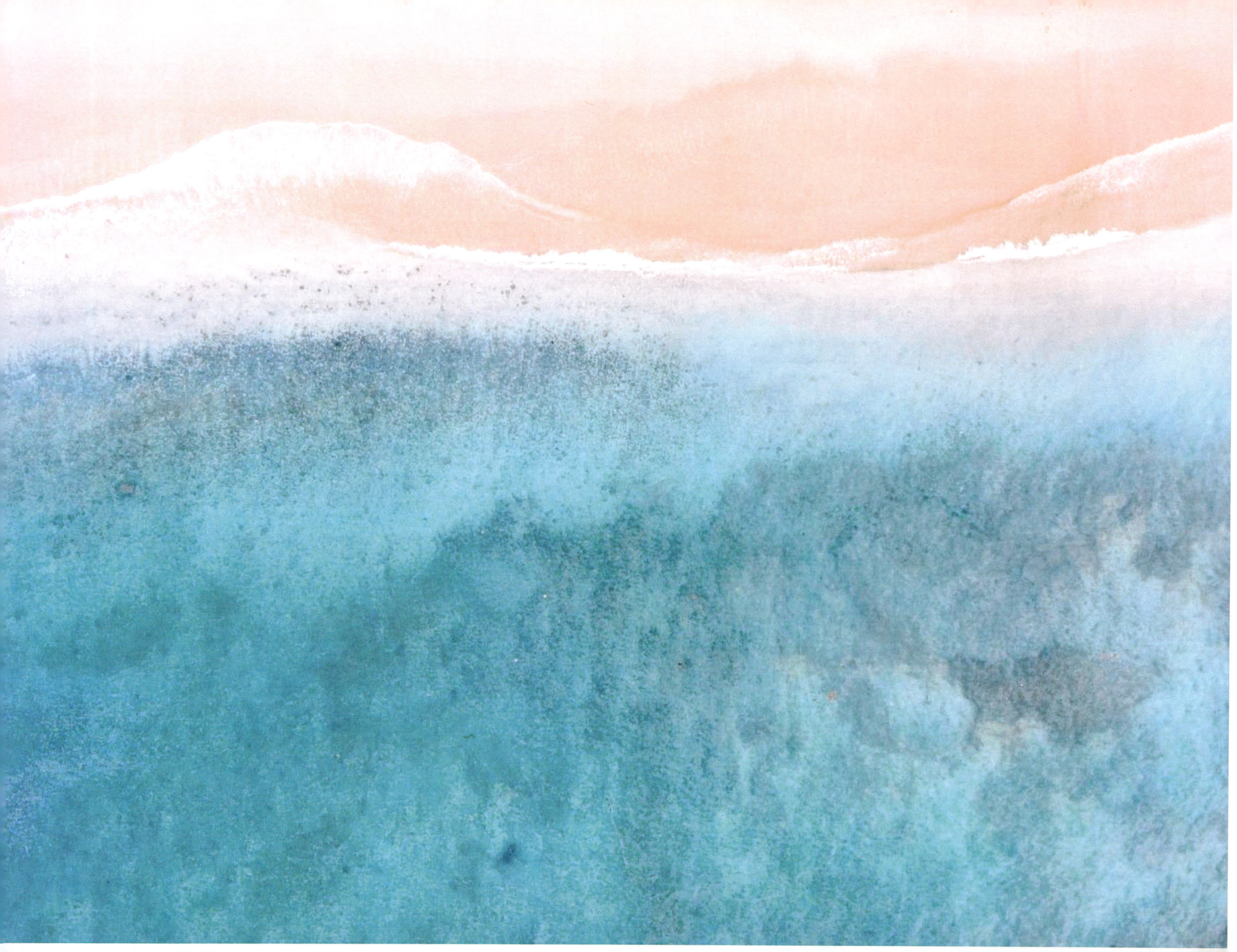

APRIL 2025

SUNDAY	MONDAY	TUESDAY	WEDNESDAY	THURSDAY	FRIDAY	SATURDAY
30	31	1	2	3	4	5
6	7	8	9	10	11	12
13	14	15	16	17	18	19
20	21	22	23	24	25	26
27	28	29	30	1	2	3

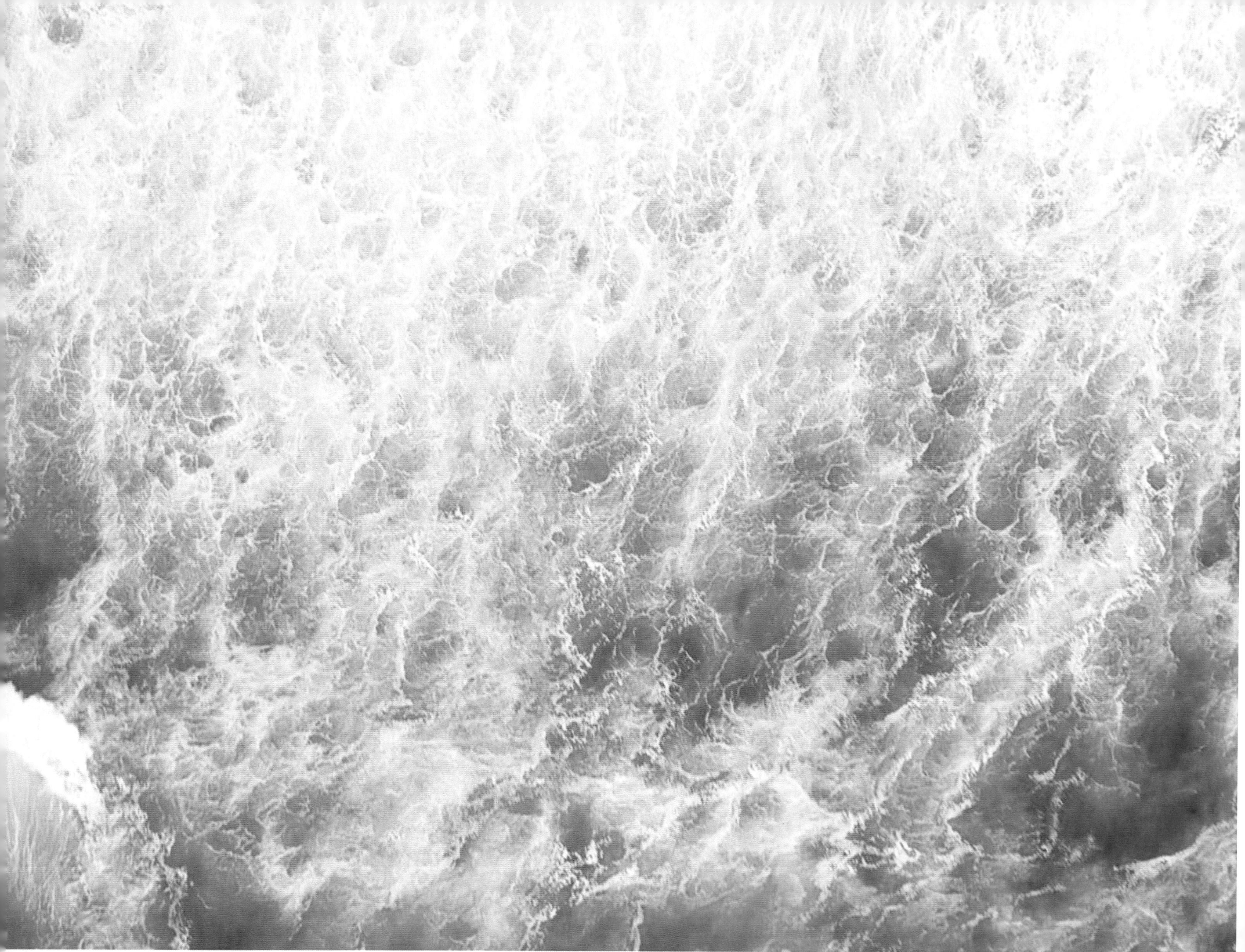

MAY 2025

SUNDAY	MONDAY	TUESDAY	WEDNESDAY	THURSDAY	FRIDAY	SATURDAY
27	28	29	30	1	2	3
4	5	6	7	8	9	10
11	12	13	14	15	16	17
18	19	20	21	22	23	24
25	26	27	28	29	30	31

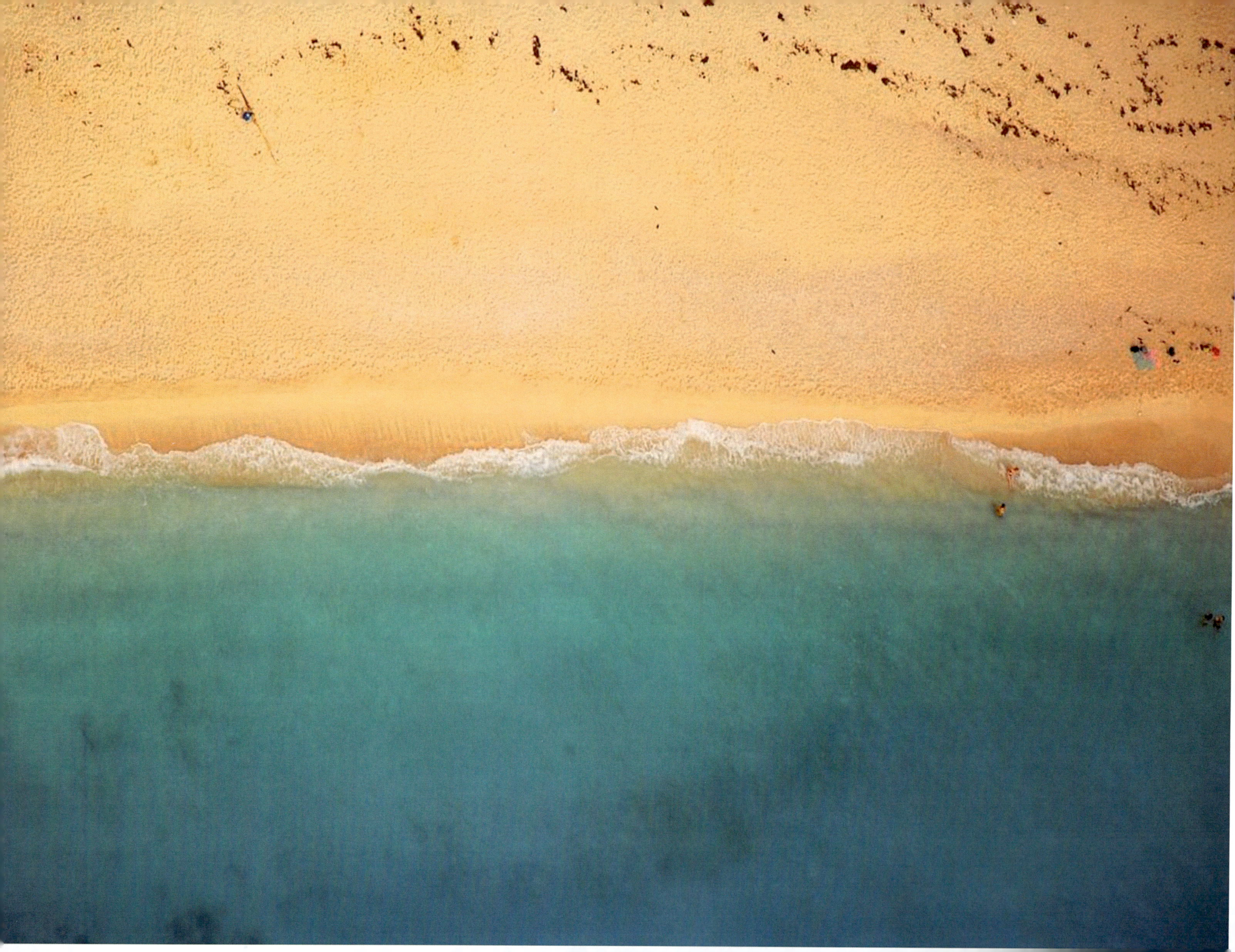

JUNE 2025

SUNDAY	MONDAY	TUESDAY	WEDNESDAY	THURSDAY	FRIDAY	SATURDAY
1	2	3	4	5	6	7
8	9	10	11	12	13	14
15	16	17	18	19	20	21
22	23	24	25	26	27	28
29	30	1	2	3	4	5

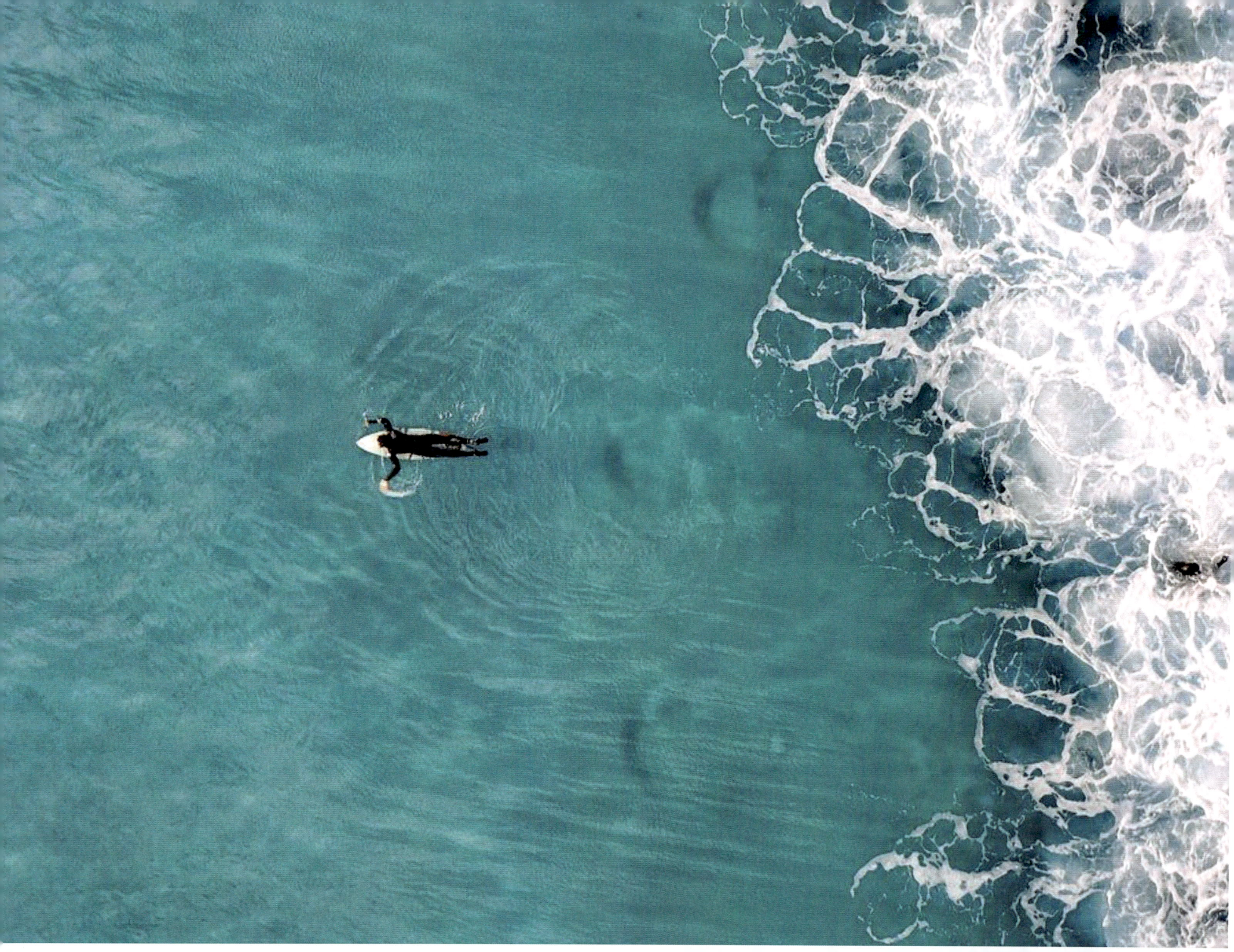

JULY 2025

SUNDAY	MONDAY	TUESDAY	WEDNESDAY	THURSDAY	FRIDAY	SATURDAY
29	30	1	2	3	4	5
6	7	8	9	10	11	12
13	14	15	16	17	18	19
20	21	22	23	24	25	26
27	28	29	30	31	1	2

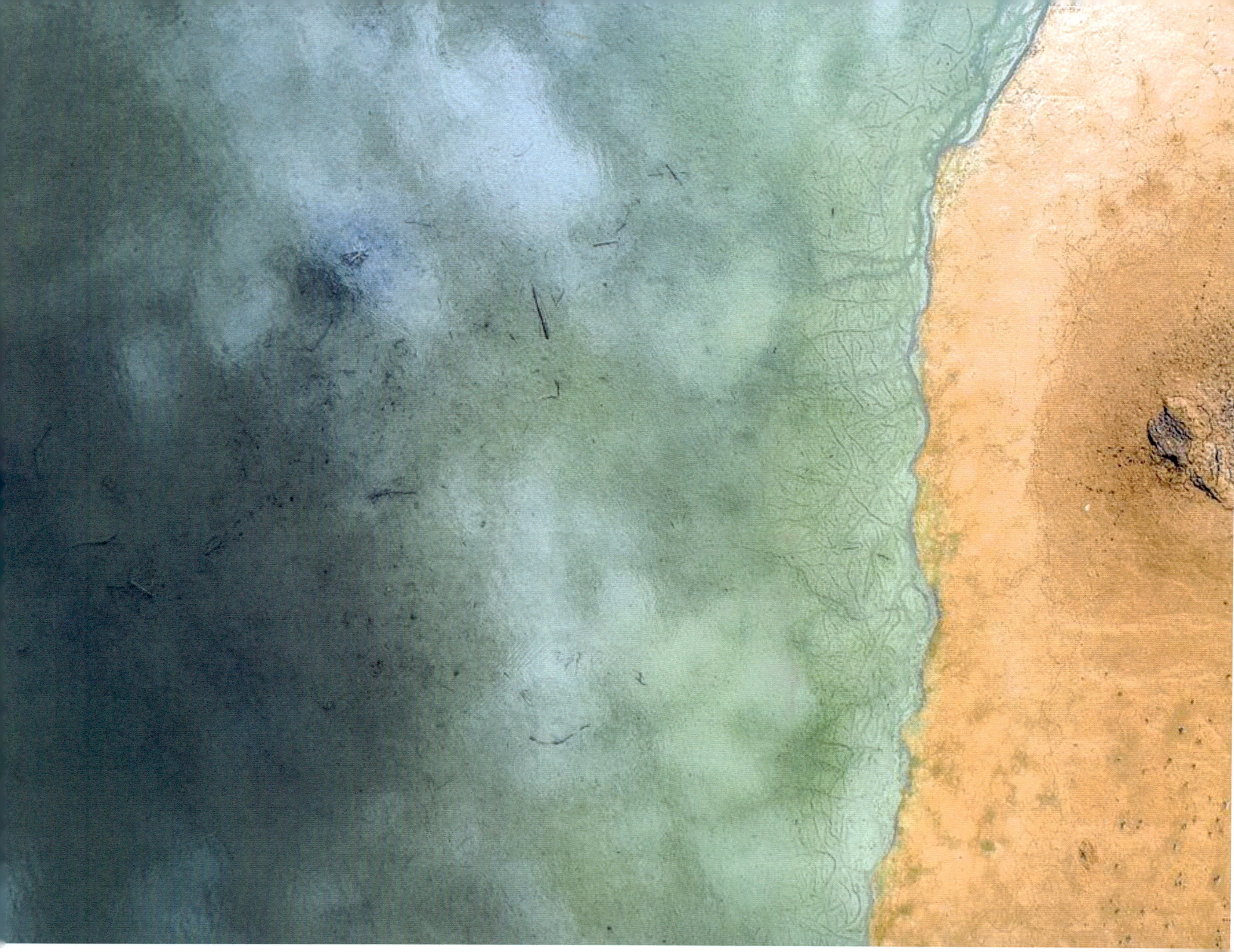

AUGUST 2025

SUNDAY	MONDAY	TUESDAY	WEDNESDAY	THURSDAY	FRIDAY	SATURDAY
27	28	29	30	31	1	2
3	4	5	6	7	8	9
10	11	12	13	14	15	16
17	18	19	20	21	22	23
24 / 31	25	26	27	28	29	30

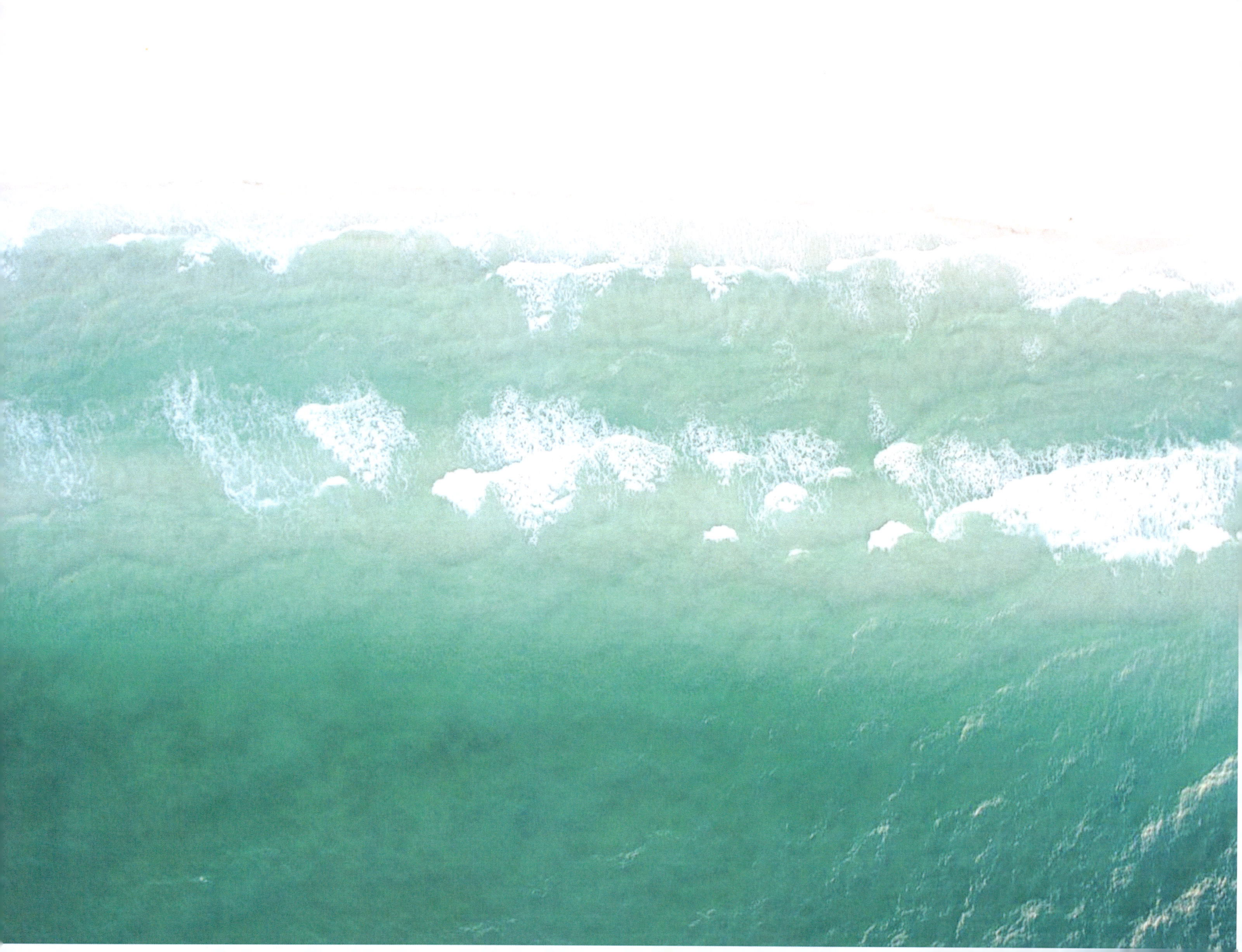

SEPTEMBER 2025

SUNDAY	MONDAY	TUESDAY	WEDNESDAY	THURSDAY	FRIDAY	SATURDAY
31	1	2	3	4	5	6
7	8	9	10	11	12	13
14	15	16	17	18	19	20
21	22	23	24	25	26	27
28	29	30	1	2	3	4

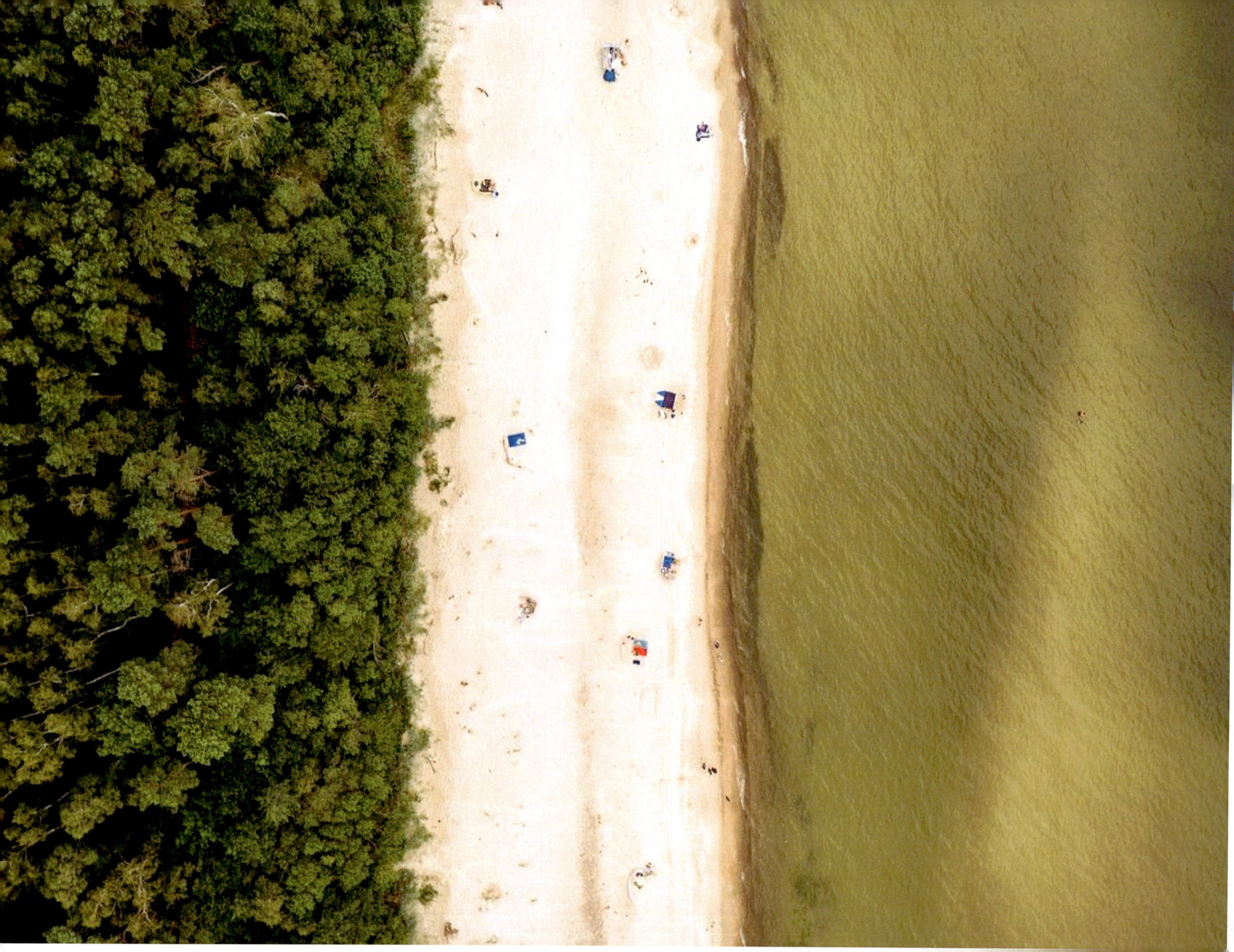

OCTOBER 2025

SUNDAY	MONDAY	TUESDAY	WEDNESDAY	THURSDAY	FRIDAY	SATURDAY
28	29	30	1	2	3	4
5	6	7	8	9	10	11
12	13	14	15	16	17	18
19	20	21	22	23	24	25
26	27	28	29	30	31	1

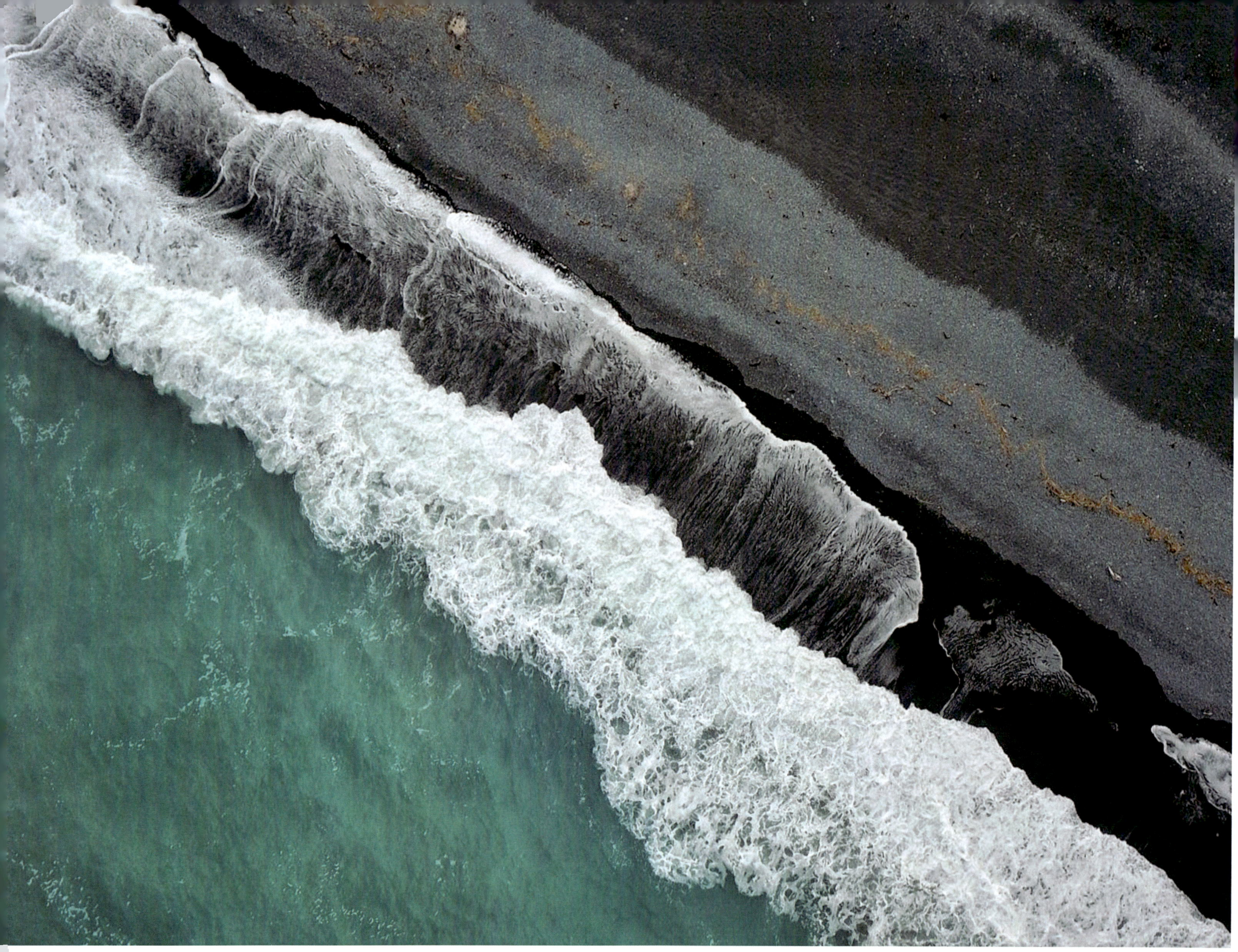

NOVEMBER 2025

SUNDAY	MONDAY	TUESDAY	WEDNESDAY	THURSDAY	FRIDAY	SATURDAY
26	27	28	29	30	31	1
2	3	4	5	6	7	8
9	10	11	12	13	14	15
16	17	18	19	20	21	22
23 / 30	24	25	26	27	28	29

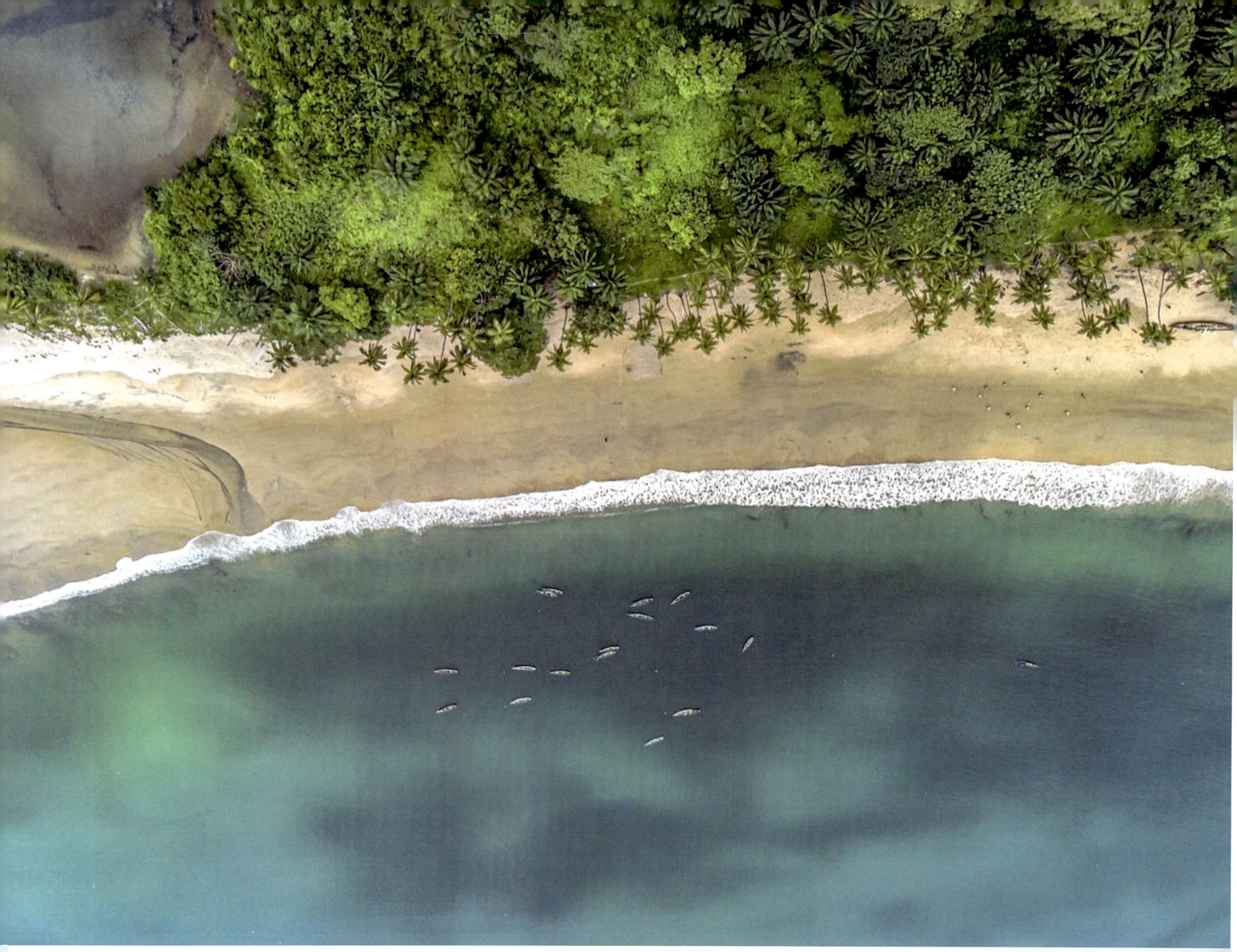

DECEMBER 2025

SUNDAY	MONDAY	TUESDAY	WEDNESDAY	THURSDAY	FRIDAY	SATURDAY
30	1	2	3	4	5	6
7	8	9	10	11	12	13
14	15	16	17	18	19	20
21	22	23	24	25	26	27
28	29	30	31	1	2	3

TOP 30 BEACHES IN THE WORLD

Grace Bay Beach – Providenciales, Turks and Caicos
Baia do Sancho – Fernando de Noronha, Brazil
Whitehaven Beach – Whitsunday Island, Australia
Anse Source d'Argent – La Digue, Seychelles
Pink Sands Beach – Harbour Island, Bahamas
Navagio Beach – Zakynthos, Greece
Maya Bay – Ko Phi Phi Leh, Thailand
Eagle Beach – Aruba, Caribbean
Tulum Beach – Tulum, Mexico
Horseshoe Bay Beach – Bermuda
Anse Lazio – Praslin, Seychelles
Matira Beach – Bora Bora, French Polynesia
Bora Bora Lagoonarium – Bora Bora, French Polynesia
Seven Mile Beach – Grand Cayman, Cayman Islands
Boulders Beach – Cape Town, South Africa
Lanikai Beach – Oahu, Hawaii, USA
Elafonissi Beach – Crete, Greece
Playa Paraiso – Cayo Largo, Cuba
Maho Beach – Saint Martin, Caribbean
Tunnels Beach – Kauai, Hawaii, USA
Ipanema Beach – Rio de Janeiro, Brazil
Varadero Beach – Varadero, Cuba
Ses Illetes – Formentera, Spain
Camps Bay Beach – Cape Town, South Africa
Nungwi Beach – Zanzibar, Tanzania
South Beach – Miami, Florida, USA
Railay Beach – Krabi, Thailand
La Concha Beach – San Sebastián, Spain
Copacabana Beach – Rio de Janeiro, Brazil
Bondi Beach – Sydney, Australia

WAYS TO KEEP THE OCEANS CLEAN

Reduce Plastic Use: Minimize the use of single-use plastics such as straws, bags, and bottles.

Participate in Beach Cleanups: Join or organize local beach cleanup events to remove debris from coastlines.

Recycle Properly: Follow proper recycling guidelines to ensure plastics and other recyclables do not end up in the ocean.

Avoid Microplastics: Choose products free of microbeads and avoid washing synthetic clothes that shed microfibers.

Use Reusable Bags and Containers: Opt for reusable shopping bags, water bottles, and food containers.

Support Ocean-Friendly Legislation: Advocate for policies that protect marine environments and reduce pollution.

Dispose of Waste Properly: Ensure waste is properly disposed of and not left in public spaces or near waterways.

Reduce Chemical Use: Minimize the use of harmful chemicals in gardening and household cleaning, opting for eco-friendly alternatives.

Educate Others: Spread awareness about the importance of keeping oceans clean and the impact of pollution.

Conserve Water: Use water efficiently to reduce runoff, which can carry pollutants to the ocean.

Support Sustainable Seafood: Choose seafood from sustainable sources to help reduce overfishing and bycatch.

www.ingramcontent.com/pod-product-compliance
Lightning Source LLC
Chambersburg PA
CBRC091244050726
47599CB00009B/990